W9-CVO-251

MORE

THAN

A

DREAM

MORE THAN A DREAM

POETRY

The Reverend Herbert F. Brokering

PHOTOGRAPHY

Sister Noemi Weygant, O.S.B.

SAINT   JOHN'S   UNIVERSITY   PRESS

COLLEGEVILLE   MINNESOTA

Printed by McGill Graphic Arts, Saint Paul, Minnesota.
Copyright © 1972 by The Order of Saint Benedict, Inc., Collegeville, Minnesota.
Library of Congress Card Number: 72-79893.
International Standard Book Number: 0-8146-0403-X.

ARISE, GHETTO, ARISE!
GROW IN PEACE.
MULTIPLY, BEAR FRUIT, BLOOM.
COME OUT OF THE EARTH,
FOR THE WINTER IS DONE.
YOUR CANDELABRAS ARE TALL
IN YOUR YARDS,
WITH PINK CANDLES SET IN GREEN.
PINK TORCHES LIGHT THE GARDEN.
THE GROUND BURSTS,
GROWING A ROYAL CARPET OF GREEN
FOR ALL THE ROYAL NEIGHBORS
AND VISITORS, NEXT DOOR.

MORE

THAN

A

DREAM

Decay has its pattern,
deterioration its rhythm
and death still dances.
The dance of death
catapulting through the wall
and breaking open space
for light and life.
Change.
Free cathedral windows
merging symbols and imagination.
Stained glass impressions
cast creatively by accidental intrusion.
Deterioration
breaking out new molds
without cost.
Revelation through deterioration.
Incarnation through disintegration.
Newness coming in the breaking of glass,
bread, and of old legislation.

In him there is no east or west.
He joins the poor at the park,
and elite at their garbage cans.
There is no malice in him.
His thanksgiving is in the crumbs.
He finds community in the crust,
and his sister in the plate scrapings.
His property is scraps.
It is his festival.
He is professor for those
learning to give thanks.

Alleys are not art forms.
They are not chapters in textbooks,
or in labs.
They do not cross city parks.
Alleys are not listed in indexes.
Alleys are not in architectural sketches
or labelled in projected maps
or recorded in the minutes of city planners.
Alleys are alleys.
The way to know of one is to live in one.
They are photogenic, often painted
and easily sold.
They hang in oil
framed.

The iron cries out for cover.
It is an acid city, active, alive
eating and being eaten.
Layers of iron chewed away
by atmosphere.
The decay doubles
and the rot runs like strawberry vines
in matted straw.
Nothing stands still
for good or evil.
Life is rampant.
The microscopic view.
The aerial view of eroded iron
and softening steel
gauged by the fierce erosion
of hard weather, corporations and some landlords.

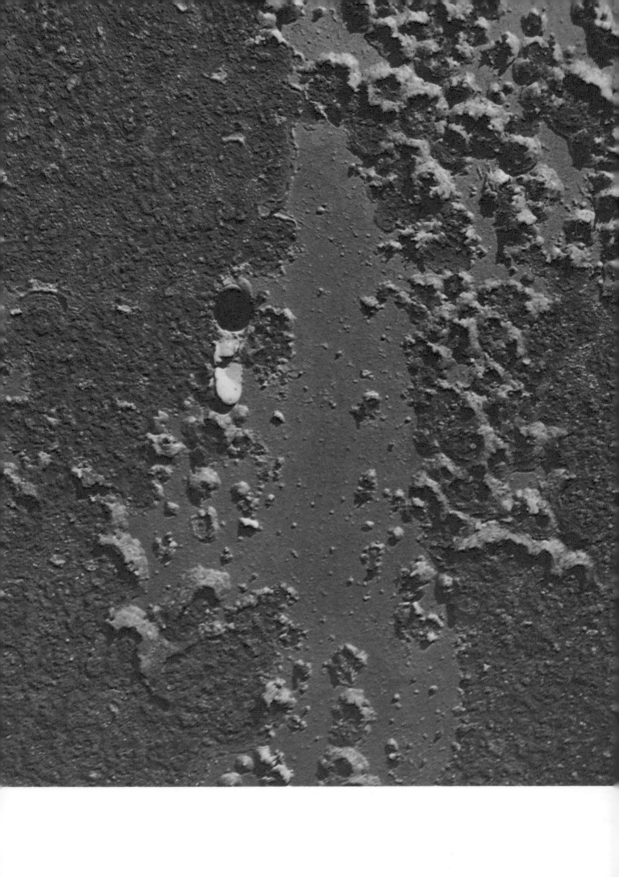

Water is for fun.
Sons of men have still to discover
and explore in fine detail
the positions of pleasure
on sea and land.
Once in a lifetime
there should be a complete cart wheel
in water.
For fun.
Show the Lord a new song.
Clown in the channel.
Dance on the wet altar.
Walk on the water head first.
Be not afraid
to dance on hands.

The sidewalk.
Where the action is.
The place to give and take,
for yes and no.
The stage for rhyme of reconciliation,
and cycles of conciliation.
Sidewalk,
where it happens galore.
Miriam played her song
and they danced.
They had come through
the high walls of water
and enemies floated with their faces
in the sea.
So they still dance
and Miriams play their new tunes
as pilgrims face the Jordan
with their backs to the dead.

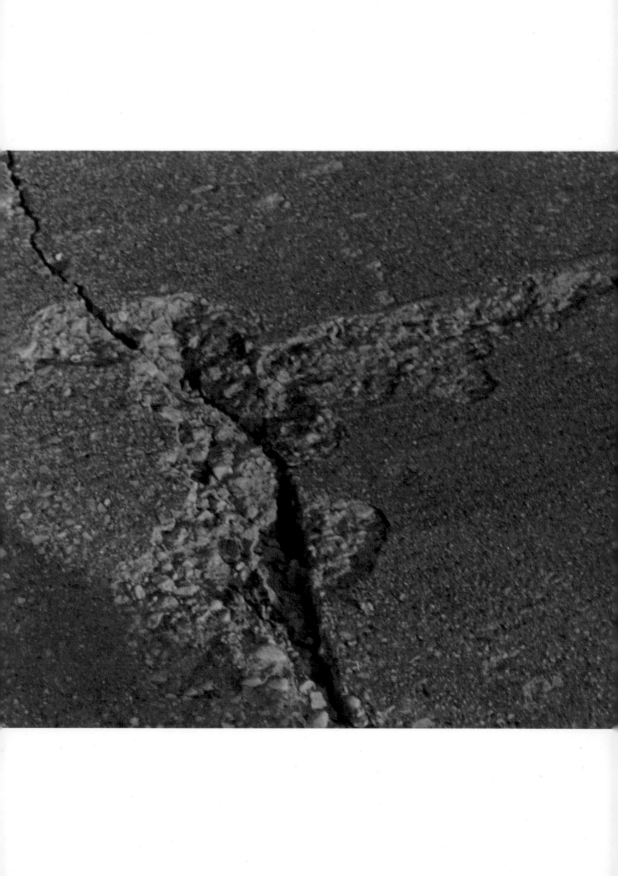

The wind has lost its nerve.
It has been robbed of its glory.
Its eyes are dimmed.
There is no view.
The light is shut out.
The window is blind
and ill clad.
Lonesomeness has set in.
Shame has covered her nakedness
and rags have hid the candlelight.
The king is barefoot.
The queen is in all her rags.
The princess is borrowing dimes.
Every pane is barred.
It can be pried
from inside.

Celebrate your body,
with a proud hand.
The body has won first prize.
Jewelry is the award.
The ghetto is twenty square acres
of winners
with first prize on their fingers.
Decoration.
Sign of love.
Sign of honor.
Sign of glory.
Solemn whispering. I will.
Loyalty. Faithfulness.
Taking and receiving.
Winning and keeping.
Being a bride.
A vine clinging to its branch.
Being passionate.
Belonging.
A sign of partnership.
Glorifying.

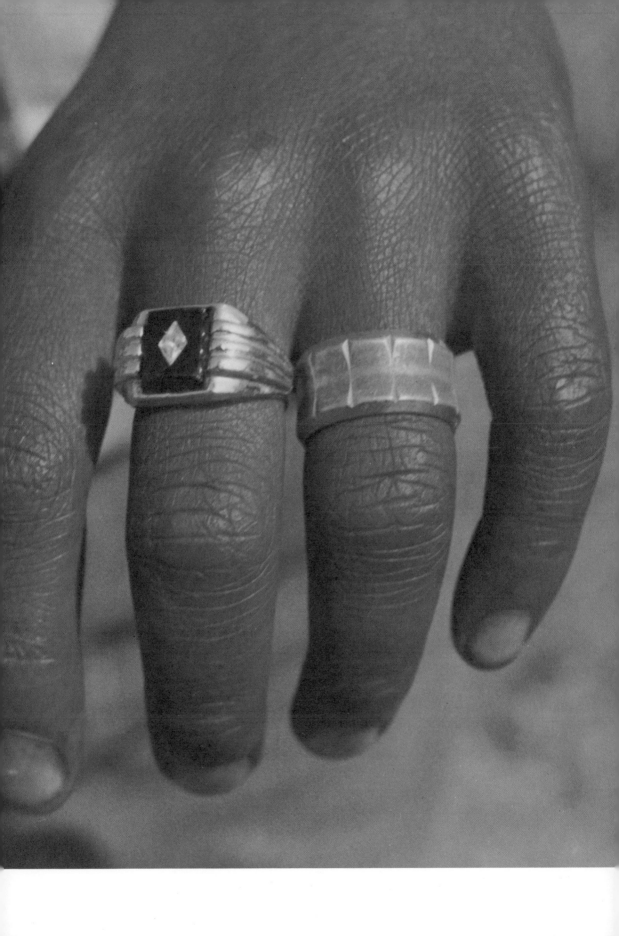

Work and play.
Peddle and push.
Rubber and cement.
There is a time to work
and a time to play.
A time to rest
and a time to take a ride.
Holiday for the holy man.
Time to lay down
steel helmets and cement bags.
Time to put away picks
and to wash trowels.
There is a time to move the earth
and a time to behold earth.
Sing and hum,
sweat and run
for men are making a highway
through high hills,
and under deep rivers.

Fences heighten curiosity.
Gates swing.
Wire is a climbing bar.
Walls can be scaled,
turn translucent,
and finally transparent.
Thickest and highest
are walls
transparent
and invisible.

Hang on.
A little longer
and it will begin again.
The iron grip is loose.
The seal is unscrewed.
The hold broken.
The cornerstone
has worked itself free,
and the systems and amendments wobble
in the hands
of a next generation.
Some bolts are tightened.
Some rust loose.
Some are pounded free.
Some lose their hold and are finished.

Israel had its wailing wall.
A place to throw its tears
and splash its spirit.
A wailing wall for exhaling,
breathing, sighing,
exhaustion
and inspiration,
and for perspiration.
How great the weight
of the glory and the grief.
How heavy a word the wall can hold.

Stone and steel,
cut down shoes into stubble.
Soles split.
Toes toughen,
building callouses for plunging on.
Through obstacle courses training for encounter.
Feet go on and on.
Straight ahead.
Head bone is connected to the foot bone,
connected to the backbone.
Feet rehearsing for peace and nerve.
Peace comes with callouses,
building tough nerve
from head to toe.

Signs have their times.
They too grow obsolete
when the laws of men change.
Signs stand flat-footed
and lose their teetering bounce
when the spirit has gone out of
the letters of their laws.
Signs can lose heart.
Old laws fall,
and sometimes their inventors
and inheritors go with them.
Laws are as new as their makers.
They are clay.
They are spirit not letter.
They are love not anger.
Green wood and not iron yokes.

The seed will not surrender.
The earth is always greening up,
and cement cannot hold back
the lunging forth of life.
Life does not surrender
without battle,
even when swept to the corner,
or when blown against the crevice.
A life against the wall
will fight back.
The law of nature
prevails.
It can be counted on.

A wild seed
has hijacked the asphalt.
A stowaway from the meadow.
A clod of county mud on the heel of a city traveler
or a whisk of wind
flying a country kite to town.
Shh. A pretty hitchhiker
is in the courtyard.
A wild orchid
for the lapel of every passerby.
No plucking and pins and refrigeration.
It is their purple bouquet for breakfast.
A boutonniere for everybody.

Green, green, the gutter grows.
Life rises from the sewers,
and foliage feeds on every lick of moisture.
The rib cage of the ground.
Mother earth is bared
and barren
receives again her inheritance.
Her rains run away.
Her land is dry under cement.
Waste returns to her
and back to its beginning.
Mother earth welcomes back.
She is the slave of her children's children.
She will bring back Eden to its beginning.
She will raise her offspring
beside still waters of sewers,
and deep springs.

Green repairs the damage.
New life in the breaking walls
is hope in the crumbling
and power in the process of decay.
Bigger than billboards.
A green gospel.
The sigh of life is breaking through
every crevice.
Seed finds the shallow graves
and covers their austerity
with soft stems.
It wears a green clown mark
to make the women smile,
while the men debate in council,
and sweat
with those who mix cement, and own the walls and walks.
The green can grow through the walls,
in the walls,
and above them.

It is the night for new shapes
and the day for new forms.
Heaven and earth are in flux.
They rise and fall
like heaving breasts.
Earth churns and skies collapse.
Trash towers
and valleys writhe and rise in cement mountains
and wood landscapes.
Passion and compassion vie
and a gentle touch becomes a liberty statue.
Revelation cycles,
descending and ascending,
in cement geysers
rising and falling rhythmically
every fifty years,
or weeks.

Play they will.
Play they must.
Play is law of nature.
The obstacle is the course.
Play is the short cut,
or the long way home.
Play is the egg hunt
in the iron pile,
hide and seek in the open.
Mystery.
Wonderland.
Place to walk long,
and put together bits and pieces
into a visual sculpture.
Play is the way to get through
without whimpering,
and to get under and in
without being crushed.
Play can turn an iron jungle
into a gym,
a rusted pipe into a trampoline.

Hide and seek.
Cops and robbers.
Cowboys and Indians.
Kings and serfs.
Seek and find.
There is no priority
in the popularity of chasing games.
Every inch is playground.
Run. Duck. Jump.
Do not throw the space away.
Doors. Doors. Doors. Doors.
Use them up.
Spend the space.
Doors. Doors,
like hollow dominions in a row.
Croquet arches
and the one ahead
dead on no one.
Hitting, playing, winning
and shooting for keeps.

He was cast on shore to do right.
The monster did not hold Jonah the prophet.
Rooms of steel and mortar
will not hold a man
hard on his mission.
People imprisoned are cast out.
Go people.
Be cast out. Go.
Get out and go.
Iron monsters
reeling in the land,
washed to shore,
dragged to land,
dumped on the rocky lots
by the command of fierce tides.
The land is dotted with markers
of the past.
There are no dates and names
on plaques of bronze.
The children vouch
like old timers
that it was always there.
There before they came.

Let there be worlds of bubbles,
fun, delicious and transparent.
Let there be exhaling time.
Doing. Giving. Making.
The people of God have always
had their wailing walls.
It is rehearsal for exhaling.
Blowing. Breathing.
Blow, boy, blow
until the cup overflows.
Cup overflow,
and surely goodness and mercy will follow
in the days of his life.
His song is in a glass.
His solo is through the straw.
His lute is the plastic straw.
He is performing
and the program calls him by name.
His cup runs over
and whole notes
churn in the glass walls
and its dome is like a full orchestral
fortissimo
in the floodlight of sunlight.

Iron crosses corrode
and cannot take away the evil.
The open sky is no longer
the dwelling place of God.
He has come down.
He comes and goes
in the open spaces
and on closed walls
between the people.
Wrought iron can mock.
Love cannot be manufactured.
The giant dye cast sign
can be a huge offense.
Authentic altars were not ever made by hands.
Altar is hand clutching
and humanity hugging
for dear life.
Solid iron crosses rise like hollow words
against the soft language of human flesh.
Love incarnate,
not iron forms.
Love has no single shape
and defies every manufactured form.

He directs the dancers
and conducts the music makers of men.
The tide and throb of sea and land
are in his ear.
He has caught their beat,
and with eyes shut
he knows the full score of earth
by heart.
He has kissed the skin of mother earth,
and danced with her daughters.
He has planted seed,
thrown pollen to the whim of the wind
and sucked its honeysuckle.
He is maestro of men,
master of women,
minstrel of children.
They laugh and they love him.
He tunes their minds to their finger tips,
and their lips to their hearts.
His world sings loud and sings soft.
They coo and they cry.
They curse and they pray.
He hears it all
and receives it like a maestro.

Calling all people.
The ends of the earth meet.
There is no longitude nor latitude
that cannot intersect this site.
There are no earth secrets.
There is no hiding place,
here or there.
Everything is a close up blowup.
Rhythm is on millions of miles
of sound tracks.
Interviews are copywrited.
War is open for inspection.
Analysts and interviewers
crowd the wires.
Cameramen are chasing through
instamatic sights and sounds.
Silence and blackouts
are against the law.

Blow, blow, blow away the storm.
Sing away the sorrow.
Turn away the dry east wind.
Welcome the morning,
and greet the world with a full chord.
Blow a tune into its face,
and a tiny melody
into its ear.
You have more melodies
than publishers can compile,
more new songs than jockeys can spin,
and tunes for instruments to play.
There are many
who sit in your first chair,
never applauded, and who never bow,
playing on and on
without a crowd.

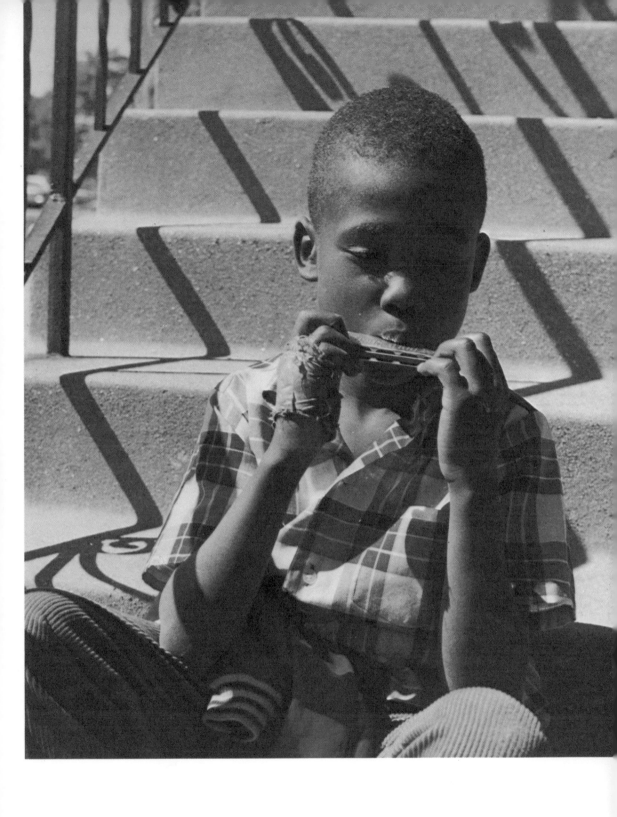

Rest in peace.
Earth to cement.
Ashes to cement.
Dust to cement.
The earth is her own tombstone,
and her children dance dirges
on cement.
Granite replaces grass,
and grass will not surrender.
Life is eternal,
and opens the doors down in the ground.
Easter comes from within.
The dead will rise.
The stone will be rolled away.
Not all the king's horses or men
can keep it shut,
nor open it.
The door opens from within,
through cracks.

Royalty marches here.
Proud pillars decorate the streets
and minister to the morale
of city dwellers.
The builders have left.
The exiles are on a pilgrimage
past ornate pillars.
Carry on.
The carpenter has done his work
and wood masterpieces
still grace the stairs.
The elegance of one generation
a grim reminder
of luxury lavished.
Father, forgive.
It is a place to walk and recall
and to be forgiven.
Wooden statues shouting,
forgive us too
if we know not what we do.

Take and drink.
This is your fruit of your earth.
Your fountains are deep,
the blossoms full,
the pollen thick,
and the branches heavy.
The vinekeepers prune,
and with the pruning comes new fruit.
Your bins are waiting.
The seven fat years are your years.
Go with the sons of Jacob
to Egypt, and return with your feast.
Famine is against the law of nature.
Your feast is inches away.

Come in. Come
a few more times.
You have helped more than your share
to come and to go.
You have stood the temper
of the happy and the hurt.
You have been the silent servant
slammed against yourself
healing hate with every jar.
You are done.
Gates are almost over.
Locks are almost past.
Cities are not made safe by locks.
They are secured from within,
between,
and in the spirit.
Not in the hatches shut,
but bricks broken
and gates ajar.

Come in; stay out.
Doors half open.
Privacy is public.
The court is ajar.
Rust has licked the surface
of the latches.
Polution has turned privacy inside out.
The lock is broken.
The latches are lost.
The wall is a frontier.
The space between rooms and neighborhoods
is the Go West cry.
Gold is the cry,
gold in all those spaces.
People have reinherited the earth,
and frontiers are being reborn.
New conquering, new creating,
new possessions and new inheritance.
New staking of claims.

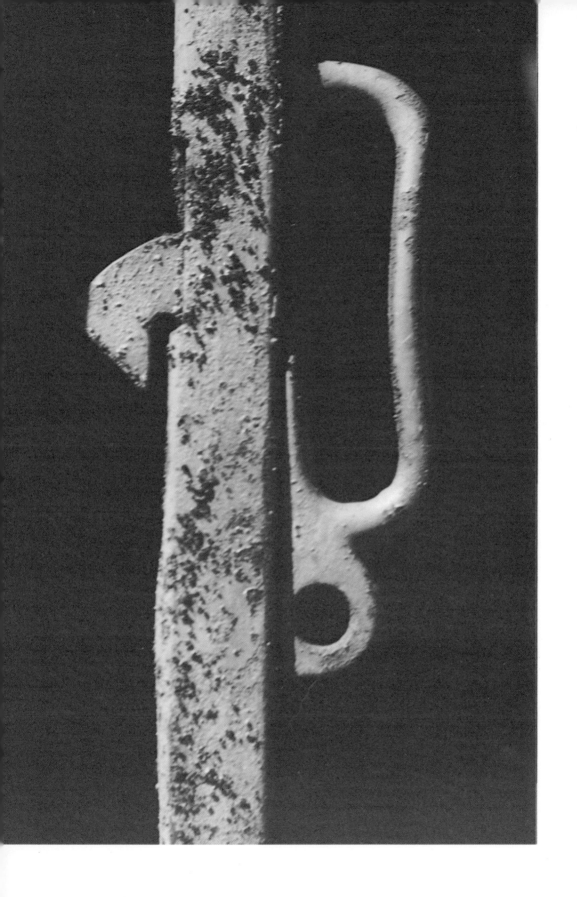

One more time.
One more generation.
One more decade.
One more election,
and then the trash bag.
The wood is brittle.
Like sun-beaten satin brocade.
Thin. It tears.
The time has come for kindling.
Oak is now tinder.
It is time for bonfires, songs,
and for new wood.
Tender tinder.
Kind kindling.
Bright buttresses.
Weatherworn.
Weary.

Swish it and squish it.
Tickle it and slither it with twenty toes.
Hurry,
before the sun and the sewer rush it away,
and bury the splashing and the running.
Hurry, and wait.
Wait for the water
to come back on the next hot day,
if not from the sky
then up from the ground.
A fire hydrant
turns the hot summer day
into a Christmas Eve
and packages
of one inch of running water
for twenty toes
and imaginary water skis
speeding behind white motor boats.

Old trophies
decorate the city.
The heroes are gone;
their records rotted.
Folklore is lost,
and the stories forgotten.
The masters have moved.
Their sons are gone
to other cities,
and have left their father's tools
sitting under shelves for strangers.
Steel signs of men,
like cast iron footprints
stir the spirits of new men
who will decide too
how to leave their mark.

They live in the walls.
Walls can be lived in, looked through.
Walls are their fortresses, partitions,
protection, penitentiary.
There is a perspective from the wall.
See down. See the wind
and the running space.
Look out of the wall.
Over the wall. Through the wall.
Look, like Moses
from Mount Nebo
and look out and to the land to come.
He and his generation did not enter,
but their children
did all walk over Jordan
and every wall of Jericho
came tumbling down.